The Snake in the Cave
Part 2: The Big Snake

The focus in this book is on the split digraphs
'a-e, i-e, o-e' in the words:

cave   snake   take   lane   inside

outside   sunshine   wide   bite

nose   closer

Wellington thought he would go to the cave and look for the snake himself. He asked Kevin to take him there.

The dogs found a gap in the hedge and they squeezed through it. They went down the lane and across the field to the rocks.

Kevin found the cave for Wellington. He took him inside. It was cool in the cave. The dogs started to look for the snake.

They looked behind all the rocks. They looked in all the nooks and crannies. They could not find the snake anywhere.

Kevin was glad they could not find it. He was feeling cold. He wanted to go outside to play in the sunshine.

Wellington sat down in the cave. He watched Kevin play outside. He wished he could find the snake. He started to daydream.

Wellington did not see the big snake dangling from the roof of the cave. He did not see it getting closer and closer to him.

He did not see it open its mouth very wide. He did not see its sharp fangs. It hissed. 'HISS! HISSSSSSS!'

Wellington jumped up. He saw the snake's open mouth. He saw its sharp fangs. The snake was about to bite his nose. 'HISS ... SSSS!'

Wellington ran out of the cave. He ran past Kevin. He ran down the lane. He did not stop until he was back in his kennel.

Vowel graphemes used in this book

ay, a-e:	cave snake take lane play daydream
ee, ea, ie:	squeezed field feeling daydream see
i, i-e:	find inside behind outside sunshine wide bite
o, o-e:	cold closer open nose
oo:	roof cool
oo:	took look looked nooks
ow, ou:	down out about found outside mouth
or:	for
er:	closer
ar:	started sharp